SURVIVING

Being Lost at Sea

Samantha Bell and
Heather Kissock

MEDIA ENHANCED BOOKS
AV2 BY WEIGL™
ADDED VALUE • AUDIO VISUAL

www.av2books.com

Published by AV^{2} by Weigl
350 5th Avenue, 59th Floor
New York, NY 10118
Website: www.av2books.com

Library of Congress Cataloging-in-Publication Data
Names: Bell, Samantha, author.
Title: Being lost at sea / Samantha Bell.
Description: New York, NY : AV2 by Weigl, 2019. | Series: Surviving | Includes index. | Audience: Grade 4 to 6.
Identifiers: LCCN 2018053682 (print) | LCCN 2018055219 (ebook) | ISBN 9781489697752 (Multi User ebook) | ISBN 9781489697769 (Single User ebook) | ISBN 9781489697738 (hardcover : alk. paper) | ISBN 9781489697745 (softcover : alk. paper)
Subjects: LCSH: Survival at sea--Juvenile literature.
Classification: LCC G525 (ebook) | LCC G525 .B436 2019 (print) | DDC 613.6/909162--dc23
LC record available at https://lccn.loc.gov/2018053682

Printed in the United States of America in Brainerd, Minnesota
1 2 3 4 5 6 7 8 9 0 22 21 20 19 18

122018
120118

Project Coordinator: Heather Kissock   Designer: Ana María Vidal

Weigl acknowledges Getty Images, Alamy, Newscom, iStock, AP Images, and Shutterstock as its primary image suppliers for this title.

First published by The Child's World in 2016.

Being Lost at Sea

Contents

Chapter 1

Alone on the Waves

Steve Callahan loved boats. He had dreamed of crossing the Atlantic Ocean in a small boat since he was 12 years old. That dream came true when he was 29. He and a friend crossed the ocean in the *Napoleon Solo*, which Callahan built himself.

Callahan decided to make the four-week trip back on his own. After seven days, he ran into trouble. A huge storm hit. Then, something, likely a whale, made a large hole in the side of his boat. The boat took on water fast and began to sink. He had to leave it. He inflated the *Napoleon Solo*'s rubber life raft and climbed into it.

Wind usually blows faster over the ocean than over land because there is less to get in its way.

Callahan had only enough food and water on the life raft for a few days. He quickly learned how to catch fish with a spear gun. He also used a solar still. Using sunlight, the still took the salt out of seawater. After two weeks, Callahan finally saw a ship. He set off a **flare**, but no one saw it. The ship passed by.

By day 40, the raft had ripped in one spot. Callahan kept pumping the raft's torn tube with air to keep it afloat. After 10 more days, he felt like giving up. But he found a way to seal the tube using a fork and some fishing line. He had new hope.

Callahan drifted for 26 more days. His still stopped working, and he was almost out of water. But his fortune changed when he threw some fish guts into the water. Birds flew near his raft to eat the remains. Some fishermen saw the birds and rescued him. Callahan had been lost for 76 days.

Other people have been lost at sea, too. Some had the motors on their boats stop working. Other times, storms caused their boats to sink. In some cases, their boats were damaged or disabled by whales or other sea animals.

How a Solar Still Works

Solar stills use sunlight to turn saltwater into freshwater. Saltwater is poured into the bottom of the still, which is usually black. The dark color absorbs sunlight. Heat **evaporates** the water. Salt is left behind. The rising water vapor hits the plastic top of the still and turns into beads of water. The beads slide down the sides into a clean container. The water gathers until there is enough to drink.

Steven Callahan designed his own life raft after being lost at sea. He named it *The Clam*.

Callahan knew most boats make it safely to where they are going. He was not worried about sailing across the ocean by himself. But when something did go wrong, he knew what to do. He knew how to survive being lost at sea.

A life raft can cost as little as **$600** to **more than $12,000**.

A Salvadoran man spent **438 days** adrift in the Pacific Ocean before being rescued in **2014**.

A person **cannot survive** past **1 week without water**.

Timeline

People have sought adventure on the high seas for thousands of years. Sometimes, these adventures become more than anticipated. Even with today's technology, people can still become lost at sea, with no way to contact those who could help.

2002 Richard Van Pham ran into a storm during a trip down the California coast. His ship badly damaged, he drifted for about 4 months before being found.

2004 Ari Afrizal was swept into the Indian Ocean during a **tsunami** in Indonesia. He was found 15 days later, floating on an abandoned fishing raft.

2005 A 3-day fishing trip became a 9-month ordeal when the crew ran out of fuel off the Mexican coast. The boat drifted more than 5,500 miles (8,851 kilometers) before being rescued.

2010 Three days into a trip from Cape Cod to Bermuda, Willie and Amanda Thorns, along with friend Dennis White, ran into rough seas. Willie was ripped from the boat. Amanda and Dennis drifted for 12 days before being rescued by a passing oil tanker.

2015 Louis Jordan's fishing trip off the coast of South Carolina became a fight for survival when his boat capsized in rough waters. Surviving on **rations**, rainwater, and fish, he was rescued after 66 days at sea.

2018 Teenager Aldi Novel Adilang was set adrift when his fishing hut became untethered due to strong winds. He was at sea for 49 days, drifting all the way from Indonesia to the waters off Guam. He was rescued when he was able to make radio contact with a passing ship.

Chapter 2

Most life rafts have kits that provide people with the basics for survival.

The Basics

Castaways in the middle of the ocean on a small raft must first not panic. They should calmly take time to think about their situation, then decide what to do next.

See what food, water, and equipment are available. There might be a survival kit in the raft. In 1972, Dougal Robertson, his wife, three sons, and a friend were lost at sea after a whale rammed and sank their boat. The survival kit they used had 18 pints (8.5 liters) of water, some bread, fishing supplies, a signal mirror, a first-aid box, and eight flares.

Items floating in the water can help, too. If you see objects, pick them up even if they do not seem important. The Robertson family found some empty boxes, a plastic cup, and a sewing basket. Inside the sewing basket were many more items. It had pins, string, buttons, foil, wire, aspirin, bags, a pencil, and a pen.

It is important to keep supplies safe. Items like watches and matches should be kept in waterproof containers. Tie down anything that might get washed away. Put away sharp objects that could damage the raft.

Without shade from the Sun, people need to drink more water to stay healthy.

Next, consider your location. Sometimes, it is best to stay where you are. If you are close to land or shipping routes, someone might find you quickly. Some people try to anchor their boat. If the survival kit does not have an anchor, you can make one. Use a bucket full of water, a heavy object, or some clothing. Tie the anchor to the end of a rope to help your raft stay in place. The Robertsons knew no one would pass by. They decided to keep drifting. After 38 days, Japanese fishermen spotted them.

If lost at sea, it may seem like there is plenty of water to drink. But you cannot drink seawater! People need to drink fresh water to survive.

Even if you have a lot of fresh water, you will want to ration it. Drink as little as is necessary to stay **hydrated**. People can survive on just 2.5 pints (1.2 L) of water per day. But in harsh conditions, people may need four or five times more than that. Castaways can get more water when a storm comes. Items such as plastic boxes and bags, raincoats, and boots will hold rainwater.

People who are lost at sea find ways to get enough water for amazing amounts of time. During World War II, a Chinese sailor named Poon Lim was working on a British trading ship. A German submarine hit the trading ship and sank it. Lim escaped with just a lifejacket. After several hours, he found a wooden raft with some supplies. When his water ran out, Lim cut the canvas off of his lifejacket. He used it to collect rain. He survived on the ocean for 133 days until he was found.

In colder climates, people lost at sea might find sea ice. New sea ice is salty and cannot be used. Old sea ice has lost its salt and is a blue-gray color. You can melt this ice and drink it.

The Effects of Drinking Saltwater

If you are lost at sea and thirsty, the ocean water may look good to drink. But it will actually hurt you. Seawater is made up of many different salts. Kidneys keep the right amount of salts in the human body. This helps cells, tissues, and organs work properly. If you drink seawater, too much salt enters your body. Your kidneys cannot get rid of it. You feel even more thirsty, and your body starts to break down.

A raft's shadow may attract fish.

Humans can survive for weeks without food. But being lost at sea does not mean you have to go hungry. You might have some packaged food. You can also get your food from nature.

Fish are the main food source. But you should avoid large fish and fish with sharp teeth or **spines**. These fish could hurt you or damage the raft.

You can catch fish with fishing line, hooks, and bait. If you do not have any, you can make them with the supplies you have. Use a shoestring or sock thread for a line. A pocketknife, a piece of metal, or a wire can act as a hook. Poon Lim used the spring from a flashlight and nails from his wooden raft. Shiny objects such as jewelry or spoons can work as bait.

When people who are lost at sea catch a fish, they must decide what to do with it. Sometimes, it is best to eat it right away. Without an oven, the fish must be eaten raw. If there is other food, you can save the fish for later. Cut the meat into strips and set them out on the raft to dry in the sun. That way, the meat will last longer. The other parts of the fish can be used for bait.

In 1973, Maurice and Maralyn Bailey were sailing to New Zealand when a whale struck their **yacht**, causing it to sink. On the life raft, they ate all of their food within ten days. They needed to fish but did not have any hooks, so Maralyn made her own from safety pins. She also made a trap with a can. She cut a hole in it and put bait inside. Fish swam in, and she scooped them up.

Surprising events sometimes help people survive. The Baileys caught and ate sea turtles that came by their boat. Birds landed on the raft to rest. The Baileys were able to grab the birds and eat them. Maurice and Maralyn were rescued after 117 days at sea.

Sometimes, there is not much food or water available at sea. It is important to rest as much as possible when this happens. Staying awake makes you feel more hungry and thirsty.

Sea turtles can be a good source of protein, which helps keep the body strong and resistant to germs.

Chapter 3

Calm water reflects sunlight. This increases the risk of sunburn.

Staying Safe

Did you know the ocean can be a lot like a desert? The hot sun causes sunburn, **sunstroke**, and loss of fluids. When people are stuck on a raft, it is important to stay cool and hydrated.

Castaways need shelter from the Sun. Many life rafts have a **canopy**. But if there is no cover, you can make one with a tarp or extra clothing. Also, try to find something to protect your eyes from the bright sunlight.

If it gets too hot during the day, you can wet your hair and clothes with seawater. You can do this as long as the salt does not irritate your skin. You can also take a dip in the ocean if the water is calm and safe.

Going up and down on the waves in a small raft makes some people **seasick**. When people are seasick, they may throw up a lot. Their bodies can lose a lot of valuable fluids. If you are seasick, do not eat any food until you feel better. Being sick can lead to other problems. Throwing up over the side of the raft might attract sharks.

Sharks eat fish, crabs, squid, rays, turtles, and many other sea animals. They tend to go after slow targets. If people are in the water and see a shark, they should all swim together in a large circle. Swim with strong movements if alone. That way, you will not look like a wounded animal to a shark.

The shape of clothing can confuse sharks. Keep all of your clothing on, including your shoes. But take off any jewelry. The shine from jewelry may look like a fish to sharks.

If sharks come near while castaways are in a raft, the people should be still and quiet. Bring in any fishing lines and bait that might attract the sharks. Do not let your arms and legs hang over the edge. If a shark does attack, hit it in its eyes or gills.

How Sharks Hunt

Sharks use all of their senses to hunt. They have a sharp sense of smell and can detect blood and other fluids in the water. They also see and hear well. Sharks feel movement in the water with sensors on their sides.

Poon Lim, the Robertson family, and the Baileys saw sharks while they were on their rafts. At first the survivors were afraid. But they learned how to stay safe. Eventually, the Baileys were even able to catch and eat some smaller sharks.

Survivors should stay aware of their surroundings. Most people lost at sea are found by a passing ship, airplane, or helicopter. Some see shore and are able to land.

Groups of two or more can take turns watching for help. Help can pass by during the day or at night. If you are alone, limit the watch time to a couple hours, then rest for a while. Dougal Robertson, his oldest son, and their friend took two-hour shifts.

When a person's core body temperature reaches **107.6°** Fahrenheit (42° Celsius), **heatstroke** cannot be reversed and becomes fatal.

Sharks can be found in **all** of **Earth's** oceans.

A **great white shark** can sense blood in the water from **3 miles** (5 km) away.

Keep watching for signs of land, too. If you see a cloud in a clear sky that does not move, it is probably over land. A greenish sky is a sign of land, too. Sunlight reflects from the shallow water, making the clouds look green.

Survivors should have their signal flares ready in case they see a ship or plane. If you do not have any flares, use a pocket mirror or a cell phone screen to reflect sunlight. Movement also attracts attention. Tie brightly colored material to an oar and wave it in the air. You can use a whistle, too. Sound travels well across water. When a ship passed by the Baileys, they waved clothing. The ship turned around!

People survive being lost at sea for days, weeks, and months. It might seem that being lost for such a long period of time would make someone avoid the water. But many survivors are not afraid. Instead, they go back to the ocean, ready to travel again.

People traveling by sea can write down their plans. This helps rescuers know when something is wrong and where to start looking.

Search and Rescue

Organizations around the world work to promote safety at sea. They develop training programs, create technology, and lobby for effective monitoring of Earth's waters.

United States Headquartered in Wisconsin, the Association for Rescue at Sea supports volunteer sea rescue services around the world through fund-raising and other programs.

United Kingdom Based in Stonehaven, Scotland, the International Maritime Rescue Federation encourages the sharing of lifesaving techniques and technologies throughout the world.

South Africa The National Sea Rescue Institute operates out of Cape Town. Its mandate is to prevent loss of life in the world's waters. Public education programs are a key part of its approach.

Quiz

1 What is the purpose of a solar still?

2 How much water must someone drink per day to survive?

3 What is the main food source for people lost at sea?

4 Why does calm water increase the chance of sunburn?

5 What can a castaway do to keep cool if it gets too hot?

6 At what distance can a great white shark sense blood in the water?

7 What two objects can be used to reflect sunlight if flares are unavailable?

8 Where is the International Maritime Rescue Federation based?

ANSWERS 1. To turn saltwater into fresh water using sunlight **2.** 2.5 pints (1.2 L) **3.** Fish **4.** It reflects sunlight. **5.** Wet his or her hair and clothes with sea water, and take a dip in the ocean if the water is calm and safe **6.** 3 miles (5 km) **7.** Pocket mirrors and cell phone screens **8.** Stonehaven, Scotland, United Kingdom

Key Words

canopy: a shade or shelter. A canopy protects survivors from the heat of the Sun.

castaways: people who have been shipwrecked or stranded in an isolated place. It can be hard for castaways to find food and water.

evaporates: when a liquid turns into a gas. Ocean water evaporates in the hot sun, leaving the salt behind.

flare: a device that produces a fire or blaze of light. Survivors can use a flare to signal a passing ship.

hydrated: has enough water. People must be hydrated to stay healthy.

rations: fixed allowances of provisions or food. People on rafts must use their rations carefully.

seasick: when someone feels ill from moving over waves. After days at sea, it is easy to become seasick.

spines: the stiff, pointed, and sharp parts of animals. Spines help protect fish but can damage rafts.

sunstroke: an illness caused by staying in the sun for too long. People suffering from sunstroke have a high body temperature.

tsunami: a large, destructive wave. Tsunamis are caused by earthquakes.

yacht: a small ship used for fun or racing. Sometimes, people travel long distances in a yacht.

Index

Log on to www.av2books.com

AV² by Weigl brings you media enhanced books that support active learning. Go to www.av2books.com, and enter the special code found on page 2 of this book. You will gain access to enriched and enhanced content that supplements and complements this book. Content includes video, audio, weblinks, quizzes, a slide show, and activities.

AV² Online Navigation

Audio
Listen to sections of the book read aloud.

Book Pages
AV² pages directly correspond to pages in the book.

Video
Watch informative video clips.

Embedded Weblinks
Gain additional information for research.

Key Words
Study vocabulary, and complete a matching word activity.

Try This!
Complete activities and hands-on experiments.

Quizzes
Test your knowledge.

Slide Show
View images and captions, and prepare a presentation.

AV² was built to bridge the gap between print and digital. We encourage you to tell us what you like and what you want to see in the future.

Sign up to be an AV² Ambassador at www.av2books.com/ambassador.

Due to the dynamic nature of the Internet, some of the URLs and activities provided as part of AV² by Weigl may have changed or ceased to exist. AV² by Weigl accepts no responsibility for any such changes. All media enhanced books are regularly monitored to update addresses and sites in a timely manner. Contact AV² by Weigl at 1-866-649-3445 or av2books@weigl.com with any questions, comments, or feedback.